A holistic business and legal consultant, Artemis Evangelidi is the Founder and Managing Director of Aipeia Consulting, an international firm focused on creating successful, sustainable and empowered businesses and leaders. Born and raised in Melbourne, Australia, Artemis graduated from Monash University with Bachelor of Laws and Bachelor of Science degrees. With over 20 years' experience across 4 continents and working with some of the world's largest investment companies, she has seen first-hand how successful businesses thrive. Now based in Cyprus, she is married with two young children, meditates daily, loves to travel with her family and cook for her friends. Her mission is to bring about global change by empowering people to be the best they can be. This is her first book.

GW00642351

Dedicated to

My parents for their wisdom and encouragement,
my husband, for his unconditional love and support
and to John, Paul, George and Ringo, for continuing to teach
me about love, faith, courage, creativity and how to live a
magical life.

Artemis Evangelidi

LIFE. THOUGHTS THAT MAKE THE WORLD GO AROUND (AND UP, NOT DOWN)

A Guide to the Universal Effort of Creating Empowered, Conscious and Socially Responsible People and Businesses.

AUSTIN MACAULEY PUBLISHERS™

LONDON • CAMBRIDGE • NEW YORK • SHARJAH

A CIP catalogue record for this title is available from the British Library.

ISBN 9781528929868 (Paperback)
ISBN 9781528966030 (ePub e-book)

www.austinmacauley.com

First Published (2019)
Austin Macauley Publishers Ltd
25 Canada Square
Canary Wharf
London
E14 5LQ

This book is the culmination of over 40 years of experiences, lessons, interactions and shared knowledge that have been expanded, analysed, processed and absorbed.

Each person who has crossed my path over the years deserves special thanks and gratitude, for each person and every interaction has been instrumental in shaping me into the person I have become. I have learnt and experienced and understood more and more about life and how the world works with each and every one of you and for this, I thank you all, regardless of how big or small that interaction was.

I would like to particularly acknowledge and give thanks and love to my parents, George and Anastasia, for all they have given me, taught me, shown me and sacrificed for me; my brother Evan and his wife Abla for their unconditional love no matter how far we may be; my wonderful husband, Andreas, who is not only my soul mate, but also my rock, my motivator, my support network and my biggest fan; my children, who have taught me the power of love and with their arrival gave me proof of a higher power. This core element of family is really where it all begins. Through our families we see and experience so much that goes on in this world and they help to shape and mould us into the people we choose to become.

To all my friends – you know who you are – near or far, your friendship and unconditional love is my guiding star and I am forever grateful to have you on my journey. Special thanks to Helen for proof-reading the first draft and trying to be objective in her feedback (I know you tried and I love you for loving it from day 1 and I guess since it is being published, you were right!)

I want to thank my mentors who have believed in me, taught me and inspired me along the way: Stefen Kourkoulis for cementing my foundations as an honourable lawyer, Samer Yaghnam for propelling me into the world of commercial law and showing me how that too can be done honourably; Mohammed Al Shahwani for proving that love, respect and admiration are the keys to building a successful business regardless of race, religion and gender. Thank you for helping me to excel in my profession and allowing me to be brave in the pursuit of my life purpose.

Thank you to my invaluable team and colleagues at Aipeia Consulting for believing in and being aligned with our purpose and for doing your part in making this world a better place.

JL – thank you. Without you this would not have been possible.

Thank you to my publishers for believing in me, accepting my submission and publishing something so close to my heart.

And to you, my reader, I thank you for picking this book up and allocating your precious time to read it. I hope it stirs your interest, answers some of your questions and gets you thinking about you, your importance and your value in this world. Let's all make it a better place together.

Introduction

"We're in the midst of an evolution, not a revolution."
— **James Levine**

A lot can be said for the way we have evolved as humans over the years. Having a general awareness of the world around us was a start. Realising that we do not live in a vacuum helped. Understanding that our planet is not a resource to be exploited and destroyed, given that we need to live on it, was another great move in the right direction.

We affect the world around us in many different ways: through our interaction with people on a personal and on a professional level, through our businesses and places of employment; by the way we impact the earth depending on how we live and the demands we make on the environment and by our ability to care and help those people who may be less fortunate than us or who are being exploited in any way.

It really comes down to how much we actually care. When you wake each day, what do you think about? Yourself for a start. Then perhaps your family. And then what? Are you conscious of everyone else and everything else around you? Are you aware of your movements and actions and how they may impact others? Are you paying attention to what else may require your action and focus? Do you know what you can do to help or how you can bring about change where it is necessary? And not only when you are personally affected but when you can see that others need your assistance. When you go to work, do you know what impact you have generally and then more specifically through your particular duties and responsibilities? Are you aware of your company's policies and code of ethics? Do you know your company's mission, vision and purpose? And most importantly – are you aligned with it?

There is a lot of focus in the world of business on corporate social responsibility – that businesses have a responsibility to monitor and manage the impact they have on the world around them (it is crazy to think that this is something that businesses can opt in to but that is for another time). To always act with respect for human rights and to minimise any negative impact on the environment. There is a growing trend for companies to invest a lot of money on making sure their products are ethically sourced, that their staff in different countries are well looked after and that their practices are not damaging natural habitats. That is of course commended and arguably something everyone should be doing regardless of how big or small their company is. Everything we do has an impact somewhere and on someone.

Over the past two decades the world of business has shifted even more. The birth of the 'Conscious Business' has been instrumental in changing the way we look at leadership, management, culture and operations. It has been a precursor for many management studies and reports on what makes great companies and leaders and how they do things differently. I have chosen to use the term 'leader' throughout loosely – we are all leaders in our own right, so I truly believe this applies to each and every one of us regardless of our roles, positions, markets or industries. We are always in a position where we can take charge of a situation, see what needs to be done and work together with others to implement a solution. We do not need a ranking or a title to be able to take this initiative. What we do need is faith in ourselves, passion, determination and love. And when we lead, we inspire others to do the same as we create an environment of trust and excitement.

There has been an increased understanding of corporate cultures and how they can work brilliantly in your favour or cause your imminent collapse. There is now consensus that employees who are respected, encouraged, inspired and who are aligned with your purpose, will be committed, engaged and will work with you and in pursuit of your goals even if they could be paid more elsewhere. Many excellent books on conscious business and conscious leadership have been written and have assisted in helping us all to understand these 'new' dynamics – new because we are only just waking up to something that should have been done in the first place, but better late than never.

I believe that all of this is incredibly exciting and of great value – the more people who start to understand the key attributes of the conscious business and who strive to become conscious leaders, the better off we will all be as people. Our businesses will thrive and the world will thank us for it.

But before we can do any of that, we cannot ignore the first and most critical step on our path. Working with and on ourselves. Only when we have worked on us, on our mind-set and on our self-awareness, can we begin to implement these changes in our businesses and places of employment. If we ourselves are not empowered, awake, aware and clear on our values we cannot possibly switch to being conscious leaders during the day and then back to being unconscious at all other hours.

The road to greatness, to success and to purposeful living begins with us. The work we do internally is never ending as we grow and change and adapt and are exposed to new things all the time that shift our realities and perceptions.

My experience has shown me that the only way I can truly help people become conscious leaders and shift their way of thinking to create conscious businesses, is by going within. This book offers a starting point – what I consider to be the most important things we need to understand and be aware of so as to begin our never-ending journey towards empowerment, self-love and freedom. So that we can all leave our positive mark on this world, no matter how great or small you may think that it is. The more we improve ourselves, the more we improve our workplaces and the more we positively impact all those who come into contact with us.

The changes we wish could happen around us need to happen within us first. We cannot have world peace if we do not have peace within. Likewise, we cannot have conscious businesses if we are not conscious individuals to begin with.

I truly hope you find this guide useful and that it at least gets you thinking about a different way of doing things. About how a shift in your mind-set will not only benefit you but the world around you.

As you work through this guide, you may want to keep coming back to this definition of what I consider to be a conscious leader and in turn a conscious business, as your ultimate goal:

A conscious business has at its core leaders who are, at all times,

- present, acting with focus, clarity and responsibility;
- in control of their thoughts and observations;
- aware of their internal reactions and external factors;
- mindfully awake; and
- able to take deliberate and intentional action (never reactionary) aligned with their purpose and values.

This is by no means exhaustive, but it is a starting point, a guideline by which to test yourself as you move along your journey to self-empowerment and self-awareness. How many of these can you tick off? Keep testing yourself and applauding your progress. The world needs you. No really, it does.

The time for conscious leaders and conscious businesses is upon us. It is the only way businesses can survive in the long run. It is the only way people can thrive in their workplaces. It is the only way to be sustainable, transparent and economically sound in the pursuit of your purpose and financial prosperity.

Love (A-Side)

∞

"It matters not who you love, where you love, why you love, when you love or how you love, it matters only that you love."

– John Lennon

∞

Love – the greatest, purest and most powerful of all human emotions. The highest energy of them all. Love. It transcends earthly limitations, religion, sex, gender, status and wealth. It is pure and simple and yet it operates at a level far deeper and wiser than what we could ever fathom.

Everything we do is motivated by love. It has the power to transform the ordinary into the extraordinary as it leads us to freedom, peace, bliss, happiness and joy. Think about it – every action you take is one that is trying to get you closer to the vibration of love. When you show gratitude, you express love. When you help someone, you express love. When someone gives you a gift, it is an expression of love.

How well can you recognise love? How well can you feel it, savour it, value it, use it? Do you respect it? Can you see how it can be applied to every single thought, action, response, event, solution, intention and creation? If you spend some time to think about this, you will start to see the overriding power within us all.

I have learnt to really zoom in on this vibration the last decade or so of my life. I have always been motivated by love but as my journey propelled me forward, I recognised the need to intently focus on it. I have used this focus to push me even further along and so can you. With love as your guiding star, you will find the strength you need to forgive others as well as yourself for wrongs done over the years. It will help you to become a better, calmer and more in-tune person. It will keep you grounded and aligned and will allow you to see the bigger picture. It will teach you how to have pure unbridled gratitude for everything, day in day out. Your days can be steeped in awareness and in giving thanks. You will be able to see the synchronicities, watch them unfold and be eternally grateful. Good or bad, every occurrence has its place as it shows you how to tune in to the frequency of love.

I can see the love oozing from my beautiful babies every day. That uninhibited, pure, unconditional love that makes the wheels turn effortlessly. Without which we would not be the soulful humans we are. It reminds me to look for it everywhere – in every gesture, thought, smile, word, tree and flower. In every interaction with my team, with my clients, with every person who crosses my path.

Have you ever spent some time to really focus on love? To observe it in its many different manifestations? To notice when it is expressed and how that makes you feel? Everyone should spend more time looking for expressions of love that are of course everywhere throughout each day. Make it a habit to look at each interaction and to note whether it comes from a place of love or not. You can give thanks and enjoy those that stem from love and start to release and let go of those that do not.

To be focused on love in all its different forms is a beautiful and peaceful way to live.

∞

"Love is the beginning and the end of everything."

∞

The Journey

∞

"Our path is sometimes rough and sometimes smooth;
nonetheless, life is a constant journey… Whatever we do is
regarded as our journey, our path. That path consists of
opening oneself to the road, opening oneself to the steps we
are about to take."

– Chogyam Trungpa

∞

Everyone has a journey on their path to achieving their purpose. You may feel that you have just started yours or that you are well into it. Maybe you feel that yours has not yet begun – well, consciously that is, as it has most certainly started the day you were born. I always like to think that mine is forever starting afresh. Where I was yesterday has morphed into today. But yesterday no longer exists, so today is something new. I carry with me the lessons, the wisdom, the blessings, the opportunities, the synchronicities and the miracles. I leave all else behind. I bring into each day the love and forgive and release the day before. And what about tomorrow you ask? Tomorrow is not real, or is it? It is what you want it to be. It will form and birth itself in the image of your thoughts and your intentions. Amazing but true.

The first day of my conscious journey began just over 32 years ago. I checked into my school's library, which seemed huge and imposing at the time and I made my way to the 'big kids' section. I looked in the card catalogue (remember those?) to find a book on lawyers – you see I had decided that I was going to be a lawyer, but I needed to find out what that actually meant. What was a solicitor? What was a barrister? Which one would I choose? I found the book, checked it out and spent hours poring over the pages. I was sold. My idea was spot on – I was definitely going to be a solicitor. This was how I was going to help people. To do my part for a better world.

I was born with a feeling of responsibility. I was always helping people, keeping the peace, resolving conflicts. I was always the one compromising so that things could move on. I had a duty to create change and I knew it.

I kept those pages imprinted in my memory. I never had to fill in career forms or sit with the school counsellor to discuss options. There was only one road and the path was clear. It was my calling – now I understand – my life purpose. Many things tried to pull me off my path but I never wavered. When I was told I could not do it, I fought harder. When I was told I would fail, I put in twice the effort to prove them wrong. My focus and perseverance were second to none.

When I graduated from law school and went to work I could see the daily impact I was having on people's lives. From the simplest of cases to slightly more complicated ones, people were always coming to be helped, supported, protected and sometimes, saved. To have that power is an incredible thing. I soon realised that I was (and am) a change maker – an agent of love, peace and healing. Can you see how that could be? I could. And in the corporate world I saw it even more so. The need was even greater there. My mission soon became crystal clear – I had to help to create empowered businesses, happy leaders and develop such a sense of trust and understanding that my clients would be engaged, learning constantly and shifting their mind-set.

The journey begins with you and ends with you. What you do within your journey is precisely what has the power to alter the vibrations on this earth for better or for worse. You decide, after all it is your journey. But I want to share with you snippets of my journey in the hope that you can be inspired to take a different look at your own.

The world of business mirrors life. Whether you are an employee or in a leadership role, an entrepreneur or a business owner, you are influencing what goes on in your business and the world your business is in, as a direct result of your journey. The goal here is to be so good within ourselves – to be in such a place of comfort, bliss, awareness and power that we influence the businesses we lead or work in so that they can operate on the same frequency as us.

Conscious businesses, conscious leaders, conscious cultures really all mean empowered individuals who have love in their hearts for themselves and for all around them. From a place of love they work through the other elements that help them to be in control and clear about who they are, working with respect for everything in and on this earth as a whole.

∞

"Before taking a decision, conscious leaders always ask: Is it ethical? Is it contributing to the greater good? Is it socially and economically transparent?"

∞

When we are conscious – awake, mindful, aligned, present – then we can influence the field around us to truly create conscious, focused, purpose driven workplaces with real teamwork, mutual respect and understanding. With opportunities for growth and amazement. With power to create good and give back at every opportunity to create more good. With increased profits and increased sustainability. With long-term visions and value driven policies. With happy, engaged and empowered people living their lives to the fullest. This is not some sort of dream – this is an alternative reality to the one that most people are living today and it is achievable just as any reality is. My business operates like this and the businesses I work with operate like this. They start to increase their bottom line, reduce work related stress and have teams that are committed to each businesses' unique cause more than ever.

So how about spending some time thinking about your journey, showing gratitude for how far you have come and getting excited about what is waiting for you. How do you want to move forward now? Doing the same things to achieve the same results or shaking things up to make a difference to you and to all those around you? I truly hope you choose the second of those two options.

As for my journey – my Ithaca[1] is always changing as I realised a long time ago that the destination is never actually fixed but fluid and that is okay, in fact, that is brilliant. The journey however has been incredible, and this is what I would like to share with you. Some of my experiences and my challenges, my thoughts on what makes the world go round and some wisdom from someone who is forever learning and challenging the status quo, with a little help from her friends…

∞

"I love the limitless creative opportunities my work provides. Being in control of your own path is empowering – you decide what should be done and how. Don't comply with rules that no longer serve a purpose. Be brave. To change the game, you have all the power you need within."

∞

---

[1] Reference to C.P Cavafy's poem 'Ithaca'

Courage

I believe that courage is something we grow into. We start off
with the idea, the hope, the vision and we slowly learn how to
help ourselves obtain it. It definitely comes with practice and
patience and perseverance. But it also comes by taking a big
leap of faith – faith in yourself and the universe.

What is courage? It is a combination of fearlessness,
creativity and hope. It is an inner pull to ignore the chaos and
push through to order. It is having the faith to know that what
you are setting out to do will transpire. It is facing adversity
with strength of character and with a smile. It is the ability to
laugh when your eyes are stinging. It may take many forms
and all of them propel you forward. Courage is like a beam of
power.

As a lawyer, working in high-pressure environments and
in demanding situations, courage was often assumed. But I
struggled a little with that concept in the beginning. In the
early days I used to hide behind my superiors and let them
lead. I was not sure why I was avoiding being in the limelight
until I realised that courage actually had to do with my self-
esteem and my own self-worth. This was the starting point.

Digging deeper I could see how boosting my self-esteem
and self-worth required me to look at how much I was able to
love myself (in a non-egotistical way). Which then meant I

had to dig even deeper and bring up all the issues I needed to let go of, to be able to move on to a place of self-love and then, courage. This was and still is a process. It takes a lot of inner work to really be honest with yourself, to find the things that no longer serve a purpose and to recognise the need to let them go.

From childhood bullying, to fear of failure, to bouts of (im)perfectionism, to rejection, to dealing with death, to losing sight of the destination, to finding another destination. Whatever it is, it is there and you know it is. It needs to come out so you can let it go or let it be. Take what you need and discard the rest. Only then can you begin your quest for self-acceptance and self-love. Which lead to, among other things, courage.

Courage is a funny thing. You think you have it sorted and are ready to take on the world. So you push yourself forward and then when the time comes to take it up a level you freeze. What is that about? How can it be? You see the journey is never ending and always ready to come at you armed with new lessons.

I can see it now – as I am approaching an incline in any part of my life, I no longer slow down to see what is going on. I put my foot on the gas (so to speak) and speed up because that is the only way I can overcome any remnants of self-doubt. And that is a form of courage – ignoring the self-created fears and limitations as you place them to one side and move forward.

I step outside my comfort zone all the time. I make myself do it. I may get a brilliant insight or idea and think wow that would be amazing to do. And then without thinking too much about the logistics, I get on with it.

That is true of my business also. I have been pushing myself and re-inventing what it means to be a lawyer all the time. I now know that a holistic, hands on and personalised approach is the only way to operate in this industry. It is the only way to really connect with your clients and help them to find real, tailor-made solutions and create greatness. I may be seen as being too courageous in my pursuit of creating a world filled with ethical and purpose driven businesses. Businesses that can support their clients and customers to increase the positive vibrations on this earth. But, thankfully, I do not agree. Making business an honourable and productive member of our society and leaving only good behind is a courageous goal but it is totally attainable. Respect for our planet, our people and our souls. I do that, it ripples out and my clients do that, then the ripple is never ending and will gain momentum.

Courage has many facets. It takes courage to admit a mistake, courage to admit when you were wrong, courage to always act responsibly even for something that you perhaps did not cause, courage to let go of blame and finally, courage to deal with everyone from a place of love and forgiveness. The last one is arguably one of the most difficult to achieve but it is achievable nonetheless.

Conscious leaders are courageous because they have learnt how to control their fears. They are courageous because they are ready to step up and lead in a way that will leave a mark. And by being courageous in everything that they do, their teams will be inspired to be the same. They lead by example and show their people that taking steps forward, not worrying about challenging accepted norms or creating a ripple, is key to creating a growth and success mind-set. Just by doing things differently – by being responsible, open to challenges, truly listening, and working with integrity and in line with their values at all times they are courageous. Especially in a world where blame and submission are oftentimes celebrated. Conscious leaders have the courage to push through all of those archaic concepts and create empowered, respectful and dignified cultures where everyone works together as a team to achieve a common goal.

Courage at all levels leads to freedom of the mind and soul and this allows you to fly higher than you could ever imagine. Freedom brings peace, harmony and creativity and creativity is amazing when you let yourself go and give in to the pulls of being courageous.

∞

"There is no chance of failure when you are following your life purpose because no matter what happens, the universe will always have your back. Let go of your doubts and fears and have the courage to create excellence."

∞

Creativity

"Creativity is just connecting things. When you ask creative people how they did something, they feel a little guilty because they didn't really do it, they just saw something. It seemed obvious to them after a while. That's because they were able to connect experiences they've had and synthesise new things."

– Steve Jobs

When I was about to launch my business, I remember meeting an old colleague for a coffee as he had flown into town for work. I was so excited to tell him all about my new venture. He was equally excited to hear about it and he proceeded to ask me what my niche was – what was I going to do differently to everyone else? I was a little stunned and remember just staring at him. Surely someone who had worked with me for many years on that many deals across continents knew that the way I approached my work was completely different from everyone else. Surely, he remembered my strict code of ethics, my different approach to negotiations, my taking responsibility for all things I could handle and the love with which I faced conflicts, upsets and problems. I was a facilitator, a solver, a doer, a giver. Why was he asking me this?

"Yes," he said, "of course I know all that. But what will you offer that makes you stand out from the rest in tangible form? How will you label all of the above into something that is unique for you in your field?"

Thinking back, it was so obvious – so clear, that I was not your 'traditional' corporate and commercial lawyer. I was a holistic lawyer and a conscious business change agent from day one. Once I could see this, making the connection was easy. And my niche was made tangible.

That is the beauty of creativity. The master key is the ability to see and connect what is there which gives birth to something new out of something else. And you can keep creating and the birthing continues and there is an abundant self-replenishing pot from which to take. It is like looking through one of those kaleidoscope toys we used to have as kids. You rotated the dial and new images formed in front of your eyes as though they were being pulled out of thin air.

Creativity really is the tool with which we turn our dreams into reality. You see it in your mind's eye and then just like magic you make it appear in a form that you can read or touch or listen to. What a remarkable thing. We create daily – you may not even realise when you are doing it. You can create a delicious meal by combining 5 otherwise bland ingredients. You can create beauty by capturing a memory on film. You can create inspiration by sending someone a message of hope. You can create love by sharing the love within.

When you look at it that way, you can start to understand the uniqueness, ease and grace with which paintings are done. When you read a book, you know the words have flowed where the connections were made. When you see a beautiful building, you can understand how the architect's hand sketched effortlessly across the paper creating something where there was nothing. It is one of life's most beautiful gifts – creation – and one of the universe's most profound laws.

Creation of anything is abundant, self-replenishing and tailored to your imagination. There are no limitations, only endless combinations and opportunities. You can create anything you want when you want and as you want. You just need to tap into this wonderful universal law that lets you do so.

I may have a thought that turns into an idea and just like that a new service is born, or a new solution has been created. Creativity sits in intangible form until you take it and make it tangible. When you think about it this way, anything is possible. It is truly an exciting concept and highly motivating.

So what are you creating in your business? What are you creating within your team? Creation brings with it a sense of power and accomplishment. Even the most menial of tasks can be tackled from the viewpoint of creativity. Have you thought of a different way of doing things so that your work can be more productive?

Conscious leaders and conscious businesses thrive off of the creativity of their teams. They promote it because they know the power in collaboration and the gift of combining different experiences, opinions and insights. They listen to what others have to say. They are open to new ideas and they create a safe space so that everyone can express themselves without fear or humiliation. That is what drives innovation and success at all levels. Through creative thought and expression, they ensure that they are solution-driven not problem-driven. They make the space for the new to come in and it does not matter who brings it to the table, for the team, aligned with the purpose and vision of the business is operating as one unit. Where creativity thrives, and fear and lack are non-existent.

∞

"Creativity is the ability to turn your dreams into reality. There is an endless pool from which you can create anything you want and live your purpose. So, create something that will have an impact – create something beautiful, powerful and inspiring. Whether you are creating in your business or creating for pleasure, know that whatever you put out there will leave an imprint forever – make it a good one."

∞

Lessons

"You can't go back and change the beginning, but you can start where you are and change the ending."

– C. S. Lewis

Learning – we begin the second we are born and we stop when we move on from this world. It is a funny thing – learning. Mostly because we learn via lessons. Lessons in school, lessons at university, lessons in life. We always paid attention (well almost always) at school during lessons. We even had homework and tests to prove that we were listening, that we understood, that we could prove we had learnt what it was that we had to. Something critical for our development, our growth, our future.

Yet in life, we do not seem to put as much effort into listening during the lessons that we encounter, as we did at school. These lessons are just as important. Dare I say even more important than those at school. Do we need to do homework and have someone test us to understand the value? To make sure we are paying attention?

Life is one massive classroom. The lessons occur daily – wherever you are, a lesson is underway ready to teach you something. In my life, I have listened to my lessons very carefully and astutely. That is not to say that I learnt – that I picked up on the lesson immediately – but that is the great thing with life's lessons. If you fail the first time, there will be an opportunity to learn a second, or a third or a fourth. Actually, the opportunity to learn will be there until you actually learn. That is why lessons have a habit of repeating themselves. Think of it as the universe's way of testing you until you get an A+.

Where you need to learn about patience, you will be thrown into situations where the waiting game is too much to bear so you will have to let it go and wait without thinking about it. Where you need to learn about faith, you will have to wait for things you have asked for to fall into place by themselves just when you thought all hope had gone. When you need to learn about gratitude, things you took for granted will fall away. When you need to learn about miracles, miracles will occur right in front of your eyes without any effort from your part. When you need to learn about letting go, you will be shown that the alternative will be self-destructive. When you need to learn about courage, you will be shown the road of fear. When you need to learn about success, you will have to start from scratch. When you need to learn about love, you will be given a newborn baby to hold.

We are here to live, to learn and to become the greatest versions of ourselves that we can be, for the benefit of humankind. Open your eyes and your ears and focus on what is going on around you. All of these lessons – these experiences – shape who you are, how you think and what you create.

Some people may 'never learn' – and that is their lesson. But when you truly understand how the world works and what this thing called life is all about, you will start to keenly look for and readily pay attention to, the lessons. You will spot the patterns, the re-occurring events and messages and instead of taking the stance of the martyr (Why is this happening to me?) you will take the stance of the winner (What do I need to see? What have I missed here?).

When you take control of the situation as a winner then you can finally begin to see all things clearly. Every experience has something to show you, something to give you, something to help you grow. When you are in tune with this flow and exchange of information, your growth is exponential. No lesson goes unheard and no opportunity is missed. That is not to say that you will not make mistakes. We all do and that is another way we learn. You may not be getting top grades all the time as you move along, but slowly those B's will become A's and then you will be at the top of your class and at the top of your game. You will be in control and in the driver's seat of your life and that is exactly where you need to be on your journey.

Conscious leaders are always learning and always open to the new. They respect other people's opinions and try to share different viewpoints. They recognise that they do not know it all and in fact they can learn daily from everyone and everything around them. In this way their teams are not afraid to share their thoughts, to share their opinions, to make a mistake or to speak about it. They will be more focused, in fact, in an effort to ensure that they are listening and learning at every stage. Opinions are not a show of aggression or toxicity. They are not criticisms or questioning authority. They are just that – opinions. And everyone has a different opinion because everyone has a different reality. There is a mutual understanding that everyone has experienced different lessons leading them to the present moment and a celebration of being able to share these lessons for the benefit of the team and the business as a whole. Think of it as a pool of knowledge and insights.

Lessons are one of the key ways we develop and expand our way of thinking. They are there to hold our hand on our journey and show us the unlimited potential that we all carry within. It is a beautiful thing to never stop learning, to never cease being amazed and to discover new things all the time. It is a wonderful way to spend your time on this earth and to absorb as much as you can of the universal wisdom around you.

∞

"Things may not always go according to plan and that is okay. Learn from your mistakes, they are lessons in disguise. Without mistakes we cannot grow. Be thankful for the lesson and take a big step forward; the path may

have changed but it is still leading you on your journey to the destination of your dreams."

∞

Presence

∞

"Sense your presence, the naked, unveiled, unclothed beingness. It is untouched by young or old, rich or poor, good or bad, or any other attributes."
— **Eckhart Tolle**

∞

Presence is something you need to feel yourself to truly understand. It is the ability to know that there is more to you than mind or matter. That inner knowledge, that sense of self that you can find whenever you really look deep within. When you are in your presence then you are also in tune with all your emotions whatever these may be.

For me the ability to feel and know presence came through meditation. I was lucky enough to be shown how to meditate in 1994, when I was in my penultimate year of high school. We were introduced to a 'relaxation' method which had us lying on the floor in the chapel whilst a teacher guided us for 30 minutes into the realms of deeper consciousness. We were told to focus on a place which brought us happiness and calm and then spend time exploring that place in detail. For me it was (and still is) the sea. Feeling the sand beneath my feet, hearing the waves crash onto the shore, feeling that mist on my face and that breeze as I would sit and watch the sunset. It was exhilarating, it was liberating, it was one of the most amazing things I had ever experienced. Luckily for me it was to happen once a week for the next 2 years.

The following 20 years were to see me delving deeper into the practice (sometimes more than others) and understanding through books and yoga, the deeper meaning it held for me.

Presence is the perfect way to really understand that the power that we are looking for actually lies within. When you quieten the mind, all that exists is you and that 'you' is not your thoughts or your body or your internal dialogue. That 'you' is your presence, and in that presence, is the key to all that you seek.

Presence is interesting in that the more you feel it and become one with it, the more it takes you deeper and deeper into the universal knowledge that is open to all. It helps you when you are not meditating in the most incredible ways. You start to notice everything around you with heightened senses. You become mindful of your existence on this planet and with those around you. You learn to appreciate and feel gratitude and trust, whilst a freedom within starts to grow. This freedom takes away any fears and brings you peace. Eventually you start to feel bliss. It truly is an incredible thing and it amazes me that so many people are not in tune with their own presence. And yet it is the simplest thing to do.

∞

"When you practice awareness, you become more present. When you become more present, you become more mindful. When you are mindful, you become more responsible. And then you become a leader."

∞

While working with my clients in the corporate world I have discovered that most great leaders meditate. And those who do not, should. We will often work on allocating at least 10 minutes a day for them to go within, quieten the mind and self-reflect. It is a wonderful gift in the chaos of today to be able to allocate 10 minutes to yourself to do nothing and just be. It then becomes a habit and eventually a part of every person's daily routine.

Presence allows you to learn who you are and what you stand for. You can search for the answers you need which are already available to you and the guidance you need from the universe which is abundant and never ending. With presence comes mindfulness which strengthens your gratitude and awareness of self. It is a wonderful thing to live your life, thankful and conscious of what is going on around you. With self-awareness comes control of your thoughts and your actions enabling you to live an intentional life, not a reactionary one.

Conscious leaders have many things in common, and self-awareness is at the top of the list. Awareness of what they think, say and do. How they appear to others, how their body language translates. Awareness of how they make others feel. This awareness allows them to be clear on their values and on how to act in accordance with them. It allows them to be empowered as they have free will over how they will react or not during every situation that arises. They can then acquire the responsibility they need to be able to lead effectively. They can regulate their emotions, express themselves clearly and listen attentively. Being mindful of everything going on around them at all times is exactly what is needed to create the right environment and culture, conducive to growth and success. Their presence does not allow them to act out of anger or fear and certainly does not allow them to shy away from taking centre stage during any crisis.

Whether you are in business or not, living a reactionary life is not the goal. You are meant to be in control of your journey, steering the reigns and creating your own path. To do this you need to be awake, alert, aware and conscious in all that you do. For corporate leaders this is one of the tools for creating a successful business – being calm in the face of any storm, inspiring your teams and creating enviable cultures built on your values and your vision.

Meditation is the key and presence is the lock – once that door is open there is no going back.

∞

"Do you know what your values are? Great leaders are clear on their values. They live by them and incorporate them into everything they think, say and do. They are the foundation upon which all conscious leaders are born."

∞

Love Yourself and Forgive (First Interlude)

As four wise men once said and will continue to say for so long as there is music and we have the ability to listen to it, 'All you need is love'[2] – within, throughout, around, above and beyond. But love actually starts with you. You cannot really love someone or something else if you have not understood how to love yourself.

It is funny how many people do not even think about loving themselves but consider that they are beings of unconditional love. How can you love anyone else if you do not have unconditional and unbridled love for yourself? And we are not talking about anything to do with the ego here. Not at all. Here we are talking about forgiveness, acceptance and understanding of who we are in our entirety.

I was bullied for a while growing up – at school I was a bit of an introvert maybe before the bullying began but certainly afterwards. It made me turn inwards and focus on my strengths to get me through upsetting events. Doing so I found a unique power – I started to understand that those words being thrown at me were actually quite false. I could see that I was something different and it really did not matter what those children were saying because I was in on a secret

---

[2] Reference to the song 'All you need is love' written by Lennon/McCartney

that they were not – I was and am something unique and special and wonderful. I have a gift that they did not have – and that was the ability to love from an early age.

It may have taken me a few years to forgive them, but I did and now I actually thank them – they gave me an incredible insight which, had it not been for them, perhaps I would have spent many more years looking for. They taught me that our power lies within us and not from what the world around us says. I knew I was capable, smart, loving and kind. It did not matter in the slightest where I came from or what my background was. What mattered was the here and now and that was the key.

So, I began to focus on me and my gifts and powers and I loved what I saw. I love the 'me' that stood up to the bullying and did not believe a word they said. I love the 'me' that was the helping hand and shoulder to cry on for so many of my friends growing up. I love the 'me' that was there to support my family and help us all through some difficult times. I love the 'me' that was loved by my husband as he saw in me a light he had never seen before. I love the 'me' that my children look up to and adore with all their little hearts. I love the 'me' that my clients rely on and turn to for advice and support with their dreams and aspirations.

I love the 'me' so much I take myself out on dates – to a dinner or a nice coffee or a stroll. I love spending time with 'me' in silence and listening to what my soul has to say about who I am and what I have come here to do.

By truly loving who I am as I am, I have learnt the power of forgiveness and of letting go. It may sound strange but I believe you can only really forgive someone when you are completely at peace with yourself – not with them. And you cannot love unless you have the power to forgive. In the end it does not have anything to do with them, this forgiveness business. They do not and will not feel the hurt and anger and pain that you feel. They really do not feel any of that at all and most of the time are oblivious to it. Those emotions and feelings are yours and yours alone and they will eat you up from the inside out and destroy you if you harbour them for too long. So, you forgive and let go while you look at the lessons in it for you. You have to forgive – there really is no other way to be true to yourself and to give yourself the love and self-respect you deserve.

So how do you go about doing this? I have found that the more I began to really love myself, everything else started to fall away or fall into place. Spend that time to get to know yourself. To understand what your dreams and desires really are. To see yourself for the beautiful soul that you are. Take a look at the people whose lives you impact on a daily basis and how they see you and your value. Think about your everyday interactions and what they mean to you and to others. Really look at your life and where you fit in to it all. Then you can start to appreciate the incredible beauty within and the potential for absolute greatness no matter where you are or what you do. Look at the radiance and the light that we all have and help it to grow and expand and fill any voids you may have within. That love and radiance will lead you to love in its purest and simplest form. Real love.

And that real love will breakdown any remnants of emotions that are no longer needed and clear away the cobwebs of stories from long ago. Stories that no longer serve a purpose other than to make you feel emotions that are not steeped in love. That real love will fill any gaps where people or places or events no longer reside. That real love will lift you and send you to a place of bliss and harmony. That real love will allow you to access the love for you that you need to set you free.

∞

"Take the time to learn who you are and what you stand for. Take the time to shower yourself with some of the love you shower on everyone else around you. Realise that you deserve it more than anyone else because you are unique and wonderful and without you, there would be an incredible void in the lives of all those you touch with your presence."

∞

Gratitude

∞

"Be thankful for what you have; you'll end up having more. If you concentrate on what you don't have, you will never, ever have enough."

– **Oprah Winfrey**

∞

Value what you have – every little thing, every big thing, everything. Give thanks and you will receive more. Be thankful for what you have achieved and for the journey and the lessons. We are taught when we are young to say thank you – thank you for my present, thank you for opening the door, thank you for my meal. Why do we forget this as we grow older? Suddenly our thanks turn into expectations. Expectations make us feel that we deserve something and when we deserve something it is a given that we get it, why should we give thanks?

I will let you in on a little secret. The universe does not owe you anything. I do not owe you anything and you do not owe me anything. Anything we are lucky to get is a gift and so just like when you were a child and you would say thank you for your birthday present which was all wrapped up in a nice little bow, you should say thank you for every second you get to spend here living the life you do. You are here to create your own world tailored to your needs and wants. What you focus on is what you get and your reality is shaped by your thoughts and your perceptions.

Therefore, it would be nice for your reality to be steeped in gratitude. It is interesting how many people say they cannot find something to be grateful for. Particularly if they are going through a difficult time or phase in their lives. Wow. Imagine not being able to see all that you have but only seeing that which you do not have or that which you want.

Start your day by giving thanks for three things you have today as you wake and open your eyes one more time and end your day by giving thanks for three things that occurred throughout the course of the day. Still stuck? How about 1) I am grateful that I have woken on another morning, 2) I am grateful that I had a bed to sleep in, 3) I am grateful that I am about to enjoy a nice hot cup of tea. Suddenly the world will seem brighter. Your coffee will taste better because you will start to think about the process it took for you to be able to sit down and enjoy it – that hundreds of people in countries across the world were involved to bring you the coffee you are about to take that first sip from. That lovely shirt that you are wearing that came from a field of swaying cotton plants which were cultivated, collected, processed and weaved into string that became the shirt that you loved and bought and now wear with pride. Can you still not find something to be grateful for?

How about experiences? I am forever grateful for all the mind blowing and incredible experiences I have had that led me to where I am today. Good and bad, sad and blissful and mediocre and amazing. All have been instrumental in shaping me and bringing me to this stage of my journey. I am grateful for it all. When I go to sleep at night my gratitude list never stops at 3 – I have so much to give thanks for. Even during the toughest of times or the saddest of times, there is always more in my cup.

Gratitude is a funny thing – the more you feel it, the more you have to be grateful for. It is like tapping into a magical spring that appears to be empty but as you start to drink from it, it fills with more and more water until it is overflowing and does not stop.

That is exactly how your life can be – overflowing with all that you want for yourself and for your journey. Simply by being thankful for what you have, experience, live, love, see, smell and eat.

It takes a little more effort to be grateful even for the unpleasant things that may occur but the benefits from being able to still feel gratitude at these times are actually greater. Every event and experience that may feel difficult, sad or upsetting is a gift in disguise. When you look back with hindsight you will know this to be true, but the key is to feel gratitude for it as it happens. And you can do this because you know it will lead to something better – whether that something is learning something new about yourself and your capabilities or opening the door to a new experience.

Gratitude ties in to self-awareness and presence in that when we are mindful we can truly see all that we have to give thanks for. Conscious leaders are grateful for their teams, for their contributions, for their loyalty and for their support all the time. Nothing is expected but what is given far exceeds any expectations they could have had because gratitude as a vibe transforms all that it touches. Their teams are more focused and committed than ever before. They know their input is being valued. They know they are valued. They feel their self-worth increasing and in return feel gratitude. It is a cycle and a powerful one at that. And it all stems from a place of love.

Say thank you all the time and for everything that you can – it is free but has the power to change the world. Imagine…

∞

"What are you grateful for today? Show gratitude. It is the cornerstone of all great leaders and great people. And guess what? It's free!"

∞

Ego

∞

"The Ego is a veil between humans and God. In prayer all are equal."

– Rumi

∞

The ego is one of the most curious of all human elements. Its sense of self and detachment from the other elements is unique. The ego knows what it wants and how to get it and is obsessed with fulfilling its desires. Yes, it will boost your self-esteem, self-worth and risk taking. But if it is followed in a vacuum, it will be to the detriment of everyone else around you because it thinks of no one but itself. For the ego, the means always justify the end so long as you are winning – it is quite selfish in that way. When you fall into the trap of associating only with your ego, then that is where you start to lose sight of yourself and your presence. When your focus is one of achieving what (you think) you want without regard for others around you, then you will be blindsided into seeing only your side of things and perhaps even causing damage to those who cross your path.

Think of the ego as you would blinders on a horse. It does not let you see the bigger picture – it does not even let you see other parts of the picture. It can only see one way and that way is not always in your own best interests. The ego feeds off fear and control and aggression. It is a constant noise in your head not letting you stay still enough to hear your inner truth. Acting in accordance with its demands strips you of your power, your awareness and blocks your ability to be present.

Instead you get caught up in a cycle of fear and anger and victim consciousness thinking that you are in control but in fact the real 'you' is not. We need to learn to release our ego – to let it go and to help it take a back seat. Our ego does not represent who we truly are.

When we start to work with and focus on presence, the ego no longer has a leading role. When we realise that there is no fear, only love, the ego realises it has lost the game. The ego is there to serve a purpose, sure – but it should never be in the driver's seat.

Something else that may come as a surprise to the ego is that you do not know everything. Crazy I know but true. You cannot possibly know everything there is to know and your opinion based on your perception of things is just that – your opinion. It is not everyone else's. So first up we should always stop and listen to what someone else has to say – you may learn something, and second, we should never try to impose our opinion – our perception of reality – on someone else. That is the ego – that is not us. We respect, we listen, we understand, we learn. We do not impose or criticise or judge. You may not agree and that is a different issue but you cannot coerce things to be your way or the way that you perceive them.

We all have free will. We have freedom of thought even when our other freedoms have been restricted. No one can control our thoughts and our perceptions. We can use our inner knowledge and experiences to help people sure, we can suggest solutions and we can even offer guidance and take responsibility to make a difference, but we cannot force someone else to think differently or even worse, as we do.

That is what the ego is trying to do all the time – take away your free will and make you succumb to its wishes. I have seen time and time again people walk away from what appear to be brilliant jobs with high salaries because of their superior's egos. I have seen deals go belly up just as they were about to be finalised due to people's egos. I have seen families collapse due to people's egos. It is not a nice way to live, work or do business.

In business, leading and taking action with the ego at the forefront is a guaranteed recipe for disaster. You end up ostracising your teams, your managers, your own partners. You end up choosing to become a victim (you could never be at fault and are always finding someone or something to blame) instead of a doer (taking charge and responsibility to bring about your desired outcome) and you spend your whole time fearing what could go wrong, what does go wrong and losing all sense of control. Working from a place of ego is of no benefit to you or your business. You create an environment of fear which in turn paralyzes your teams and leads to more fear and mistakes and miscommunication. People are scared to speak up and be heard and will try to avoid engaging at all costs. This is not how conscious leaders do business – in fact it is the exact opposite.

Let your ego go. Stop trying to control, change, influence and make people do things your way. Work from a level of respect, understanding, trust and love. Learn to listen, to share and experience what others are saying and doing. Learn to work with people not against them.

The ego has no place in business, it has no place in family and it has no place amongst friends. Do not feed its fear and aggressiveness. Learn to work with it in a peaceful way so you keep the benefits of what it can offer, but not without context. In this way it will be slowly pushed to the back, activated only in those circumstances where it can really add value and not to trivialise your real power – that which is found in pure, unconditional love.

∞

"Great people and great leaders learn from the people around them. They know when to ask the right questions, are quiet long enough to really listen and welcome ideas and solutions from the knowledge base available to them within their circles and within their organisations."

∞

Fear

∞

"The only thing we have to fear is fear itself."
— **Franklin D. Roosevelt**

∞

Fear – ego's partner in crime. What better way to control you and stop you in your tracks than to introduce this concept. Fear is everywhere – it is like a drug, a tool to control your mind and keep you submissive. Just turn on the evening news. Fear, fear and more fear. Fake news, fake fears and fake realities. And the more you watch, the more you start to think it may be true. So, you start to live according to someone else's schedule and program. You buy things you do not need so you can be 'safe'. You cancel that holiday so you can avoid any impending danger. You do not take that next big leap so you do not fail.

Fear of failure, of success, of taking responsibility, of life, of death, of anything and everything. It is a powerful tool. And it is an emotion that needs to exit your life right now. Fear is nothing but a thought about something that has not yet occurred and does not, in fact, exist. It is a thought about a potential outcome. Instead of focusing on that outcome, shift your thoughts so you focus on another outcome. Given that all outcomes are possible, why not create the one you want?

Leaders who are ready to take on the world stare fear straight in the eyes and then tell it to move on. It has no place in their lives. Likewise, for anyone in the world of business, if we listened to fear we certainly would not get very far. We would never have left our last job or taken that leap of faith into the unknown. Fear is debilitating. It stops you dead in your tracks frozen like a deer in the headlights. Surely that is no way to live.

No – fear has no place in an empowered life. You cannot live in the present when you are constantly living in the future and the future does not exist. You are so busy worrying about what could be that you forget to worry about what is.

What is the best way to deal with your fears? Well I have a process that I find actually works quite well. First, you identify exactly what it is that you are afraid of – let us say, by way of example, that it is a fear of speaking in public. Second, you start to break down the fear by really thinking about and listing what it is that scares you about speaking in public. What is the thought process leading to the fear? That you will have to stand up in front of people; that you will have to remember what to say; what if the crowd is not engaged; what if you are not able to connect with them; what if you lose your train of thought; what if the projector does not work… you get the idea. Third, you find a solution for each thought. Okay, so you are standing up in front of people who have actually come to hear you speak – that is a good thing not a bad thing! They are already happy to be there. You need to remember what to say – but you have your presentation and your written prompts in front of you. And anyway, even if you forget the next part you will always find a way to ad lib and fill in the gaps. There is no way that they will not be engaged, because you know that your talks are always interesting and amusing and full of useful information. Fourth, you start to visualise your desired outcome. So, you are standing up on stage, you are looking down at happy smiling faces, you feel very calm and in control, you start to speak and the words flow effortlessly and you remember every part and every light-hearted joke. You are speaking at the ideal pace, everyone is engaged and before you know it, it is over and you step back to your seat with a round of applause feeling happy and satisfied.

You will then keep this visualisation with you and go through it as much as you can leading up to the talk. And then when you get up on stage, you will feel that you have already done this so many times, that it is as though you are repeating an event that has transpired. It flows, it is over and it felt like absolutely nothing. What was all that stress and worry about? What were you so afraid of – it really was not a big deal.

This is a great exercise to try. The beauty of it is that it can be applied to any fear you have about anything. I really enjoy doing this exercise with my clients – leaders, their teams, entrepreneurs. We work through the four-step process together, breaking it down in the second step as far as we can go and then working through the solutions on a whiteboard. It really helps to see how insignificant a fear becomes when you write it down.

Conscious leaders cannot allow fear to govern how they operate. They cannot be afraid to lead in the manner that they do; to take ownership of problems and find solutions; to try out different ways of doing things; to put themselves in control of situations and outcomes. Fear would result in them reverting to the role of the victim where everything is occurring to them and they would lose their ability to control events or affect the way in which they transpire.

Do not let your life and all the things you would love to do, fall away because of fear. Remember that it is not something concrete – it is a thought – and just like all thoughts, you can dismantle it and push it away. When you are in control of your thoughts you can catch the ones that start to make you feel anxious or stressed and pinpoint the source of fear around them. And then you can get rid of them so you can live your life just as you want to – to do all the things you have dreamt of doing and to experience everything that is on offer. Live without regrets and without fear.

∞

"Are you a victim or a doer? Victims are disempowered and go through life throwing blame around. Doers always stand firm in their power, take ownership of the problem and know that they can shape the future regardless of what is going on around them. Fear has no place in a doer's life."

∞

Conflict

∞

*"When conflicts arise, step away and breathe. There's a
natural universal law that when you change the vibration
of something, you change the result. The natural response
is to fight back, which only increases the 'vibration' of the
conflict, but inner stillness in one person changes the
result for both people. Just try it and see!"*
— **Renee Miller**

∞

Whether we like it or not, life is full of conflicts. Internal
conflicts and external ones. Conflicts between people,
conflicts between nations. They are all around us and often
times a part of our daily lives.

As with everything else, we always start with ourselves
when it comes to conflict. When we are dealing with an inner
conflict we need to brainstorm to figure out what it is that we
cannot decide on. Just as with fear, break it down and then
create a list of the pros and cons. Work through the process
just as you would a negotiation with a third person. Our inner
conflicts have the power to hold us back and keep us frozen
in time, much like fear does. That is why it is so important
that they be worked through and dealt with quickly. You do
not want to be wasting time in limbo.

However, our inner conflicts also offer us something
positive — an insight into who we really are and what makes
us tick. Remember everything that happens is a lesson in
disguise — an opportunity to learn something new. Our inner
conflicts are a window to our values and this window is the
perfect opportunity to dig deep and see what our values really
are.

We all have a set of values that we hold dear and that guide us through life. These are our personal non-negotiable red lines. Things like integrity, ethics, trust, commitment, open communication. These form the foundation of our personality and our overall presence. Being true to them at all times is what keeps our inner conflicts to a minimum.

∞

"Acting with integrity is by far one of the most beautiful and admirable of all human traits. Create your culture around your values. Like attracts like."

∞

External conflicts on the other hand are when we are faced with an outside challenge to our values. But these too can be easily resolved. In fact, we can control any conflict and bring about an outcome that is acceptable to all the parties involved, simply by taking charge and steering the conflict where we want it to go, in line with what we value.

The first rule is to act with respect, honesty and transparency – values most of us already hold dear. Whether your conflict is with a friend, sibling or a colleague or you are in the throes of negotiating an important transaction or trying to bring on board a new employee, the same rules apply. Do not lie and do not withhold crucial information as a tactic to get your way. The second rule is to be clear on what you want to achieve – what your desired outcome is. That means that you will then be willing to compromise on those things that are not as crucial for you. You know where your red lines are and what is a deal breaker. Therefore, if something does not mean much to you but means the world to someone else, do not hoard it just to prove a point or to prove your power. That is the ego at work and as we already know, that will not lead to a good outcome. Compromise where you can and remember that the end result is for all parties to walk away happy.

Open and true communication is so important. Speak truly and listen deeply. Express yourself – your truth – what you want and why and do not hold things back. People are not mind readers so unless you let people know what you are thinking and what you want to achieve they will not be able to support you. The flip side to this is that you must also listen to what people are saying. Do not interpret what others say to fit into your reality but make a conscious effort to see things from their perspective and step into their shoes to feel as they do. When you speak and when you listen do so from a place of respect and unconditional love. This is the key to open and true communication. Do not blame, do not get angry and do not argue. Express and listen. Self-awareness here is key so you can catch yourself when your thoughts become critical or negative. If and when they do, you need to notice and remember that you are trying to resolve a conflict – not create another one.

Conscious leaders know to practice all of this with integrity. Acting with integrity in everything that they do and particularly when trying to resolve conflict is non-negotiable (pardon the pun). Integrity is one of our most beautiful virtues and it is what helps to dissolve conflict together with true and open communication, compromise and acting from a place of love. It also keeps them in line with their other values at all times as they move through the conflict working towards a resolution. As a result of this, their word is their honour. There is no room for white lies nor is there room for not keeping their promises. A leader who follows through on what was spoken gains the trust and respect of their teams. There is power in the spoken word and there is even more power in its honest and truthful implementation.

∞

"True leaders are in control of their thoughts, are constantly observing their surroundings and are never reactionary. They foster respect and trust and create a culture in their mirror image."

∞

Time

Time is a funny thing. Sometimes we are in the flow with it, other times it gets the better of us. I am not talking about 'managing time' like a business training concept but being one with time – working with it and using it to your benefit.

A lot of people have a love/hate relationship with time – we are angry at it for taking things away from us we cannot get back and anxious for it to bring us what we want, when we want it. This of course does not always go to plan and we end up being out of sync with time and ourselves and all that that means.

We know from the great Albert Einstein that time is relative – it is relative to the observer and more specifically to the motion of that observer. According to the theory of relativity, our perception of a 'now' that flows as it moves along in time, is actually a result of human consciousness. There is no fixed frame of reference in the universe – everything is moving relative to everything else. Time passes at a different rate for each observer who is travelling at different speeds – an example of this is that two clocks that were previously synchronised, cannot stay synchronised if they move relative to each other at different speeds. Another example is that a fast-moving observer would measure time passing slower than a stationary observer would. This is what Albert Einstein called 'time dilation'.

As we also know, time and space go hand in hand – they form a part of one continuum called space-time within which all objects are located and all events occur.

In lay person's terms that sort of means that to me, time will move differently than what it does to you according to what we are doing and how we perceive it at any given time. Have you ever had days where you feel as though time is moving slowly and you accomplish so much and then other days, time moves so quickly you cannot believe it has gone? I have that every day and I may announce it in the office "Wow today has flown" and someone will always pipe up and say, "Really? No, for me it is really moving so slowly today."

So why does this matter to us on our quest to becoming empowered and conscious individuals and leaders? Time is everything – we need to understand it and respect it and be in the flow with it regardless if it is just our perception of it that we can measure. Time is a way of measuring the passing moments and each moment that passes leaves behind an imprint. So how we utilise that 'time' and how we plan for things in the future is very important.

Plan your journey, focus on your goals and work towards them daily, persistently and with a time line in place, of course. But this time line will waiver and change as you move along because time is not something fixed but it is forever moving and changing and adapting to you and your reality.

We should not place unrealistic expectations on ourselves or others. Remember that the journey is one laden with lessons, opportunities and room for change and growth. Time adapts with all of this and moves along with you. Do not be angry at time when something you wanted to have happen yesterday has not transpired yet. Instead have faith and look carefully at what time is trying to tell you. You may not be ready for it or maybe the timing in general is off because something else is about to happen that you were not aware of.

Hindsight is a wonderful thing – it allows you to truly understand what has happened and why and have your 'aha' moment, but until then do not push things that do not want to be pushed. Keep your head down, your focus unwavering and work towards your goals but show respect for time and remember that it is working with you, not against you.

Timing is another interesting element of time. 'Timing is everything' they say. We have heard it so many times but have we ever given real thought to what it means? My thoughts on this are as follows. Given that time and space are linked and time is relative to where you are right now in this moment and where you are going, whether something will work out in your favour or as you expect it to, has more to do with where you are in the space-time continuum than what your intentions are. Every action has a reaction and whilst our intentions may give us clarity on what we want to achieve, we do not live in an isolated vacuum. We do live in a universe with complex laws of physics which govern our every movement and even our every thought (quantum physics is a captivating, often mind-boggling area but I will leave that to the experts). So, whilst you may intend for one thing to go this way, at this moment in time, maybe it can only go the other way. When circumstances change, which relies on factors often out of your control, the situation may suddenly go your way. And that is when we say, 'timing is everything'. When you have this in mind, you can see that so-called failures are not failures at all – they are in fact telling you that right now is not the best time for this to happen. Or it could be done in a different way, but later on. And your intention remains the same and your desires resolute but you shift your expectation to another moment in time.

Fascinating, yes? Why not think back to an event in your life that may not have transpired when you wanted it to, but after a while it suddenly appeared on your doorstep as though by magic? What changed? Not your intentions or attempts to get at it. The external circumstances – most probably. Time – with absolute certainty.

∞

"Things didn't go as planned? Look closely – there is a lesson in it for you. Learn from it, show gratitude and keep moving forward. The past no longer exists, the future is yours for the taking."

∞

Love Energy (Second Interlude)

∞

"Love is real, real is love, love is feeling, feeling love."
— **John Lennon**

∞

The power of love is sometimes incomprehensible. Incomprehensible in that it holds so much energy that it can literally change the world. It is the highest vibration there is. When you are aware of its power you can really see how using it liberally and daily can transform your every action and interaction.

When we talk about approaching everything you do with love we mean that regardless of what you are doing, where you are doing it and why you are doing it, you can always approach a situation from this standpoint. It will dissolve the anger, stress and anxiety that may have crept up on you while you were trying to resolve a problem. It will ease the tension you feel when you are about to step up in front of a crowd to speak. It will make people calmer when you need to announce difficult news. It is about using the energy of the feeling that love creates to change the vibration around you. It is the only real thing there is.

Love is everything – it is the sound, the sight, the touch, the smell, the feeling, the breath, the thought, the beat of your heart. It is the energy that fuels everything else. It has the remarkable power to wipe out grief, fear, anger, sadness, stress, anxiety and anything else vibrating lower than it, in an instant.

Close your eyes for a moment – whatever you are doing, just stop and imagine that someone you truly care for is right there next to you and is giving you a big hug. A long, warm, loving big hug. What is the sensation that rushes through your body? The sense of euphoria, calm and knowledge that everything will be alright. That is the energy of love spreading through you from a single physical representation of the emotion. If you have ever had a child come and hug you, that feeling you just imagined is multiplied infinitely. The love from a child, pure, innocent and unconditional, is one of the strongest vibrations you will ever encounter in this lifetime.

So why do we find situations where expressing and working with love is acceptable and others where we feel as though it is inappropriate? Whoever said that love can be switched on and off depending on the circumstances as if there is such a switch to begin with?

Love cannot be switched on and off – either you come from a place of love energy in all that you do or you do not. When you go to work – how you speak to your colleagues is a reflection of the energy you are vibrating on. Are you respectful and considerate? That is from the love energy. Are you rude and abrupt? That is from the ego and lower vibrations that are not helping you to evolve and become an empowered and conscious human being.

From a leadership perspective, conscious leaders feel love for their teams, they work from a place of love at all times and they utilise this energy in all that they do regardless of the context. So, a meeting, finalising a transaction, completing a merger or solving a staffing problem does not make a difference to the approach. It all begins from a place of love – respect, open communication, trust and transparency. Keeping it at this level assists you more than you can imagine. Yes, you will fight for what you want, you will be firm and level headed, you will aim to achieve the best deal for you and your company and your teams but when you do all this from a place of love, you can achieve more and make things work for you whilst keeping things pleasant.

Love energy is pure white energy clean and simple. And given that energy makes up the world we live in, including ourselves, we need to be vibrating on this pure white energy at all times in order to be in tune with ourselves and the world around us.

Things that bring us pleasure are not created from a place of hate or misery. Nothing can grow from a foundation of anger or rudeness. Greatness cannot transpire from a lack of respect or lies. Beautiful, life changing and inspiring things all grow from a place of pure unconditional love energy. Think relationships, art, music, poetry, books, theatre, responsible businesses that last the test of time. Love sits behind all these things, supporting and holding them up with its purity and expecting nothing in return.

Think about how all the other emotions make you feel, how long they linger and how you respond as a result of them. List them and go through each emotion one by one. Then think of love. How it makes you feel. Close your eyes and savour it. There really isn't anything like it.

∞

"Conscious businesses cannot operate within a loveless void. Love is the undercurrent of all great things. Conscious leaders know that love is one of the core elements of their being, one of their principal values and the only way they can create conscious cultures that thrive."

∞

Bravery

"Bravery is not a quality of the body. It is of the soul."
                                    — **Mahatma Gandhi**

Without bravery we cannot get a lot done, much like courage. Whilst courage helps you achieve your goals in the face of your self-conceived fears, bravery allows you to step up in the face of real risk or danger. Think of it as taking your courage to another level.

Being brave means different things to different people. For you it could mean taking that next step in your career and trying something that has never been done before. It could also mean pushing yourself and testing your own boundaries to see how quickly you can adapt and adjust and move in a different direction with something new.

I believe that bravery cannot function in a vacuum – in order to be brave you have to also master something else – responsibility. Full and unconditional responsibility, both for your actions and for the actions of others. It may sound strange but taking responsibility wherever you can is actually one of the first things empowered and conscious leaders do at all times.

When you take a brave step forward – whether at work, or in a relationship – you must also be ready to take the heat for what you are about to do and how it may affect others. Whilst you cannot control what others say, think and do, and to be honest, you do not want to anyway, if your actions bring about any sort of reaction in anyone else, you have to step up and take responsibility for this. Regardless whether the other person should have done something to lessen the damage or could have spoken or acted in a different way. That leads you to blame and blame does not provide any solace or any growth. Blame leads to regret and anger and puts you in the role of the victim.

A brave person is never a victim. They are always a doer and the doer does not shy away from responsibility. A victim believes that everything that happens is ultimately someone else's fault and that they have no control over external circumstances. As a result, they are not accountable for what has happened nor can they offer any solutions because, well everything that has happened is out of their control. That does not sound very brave now does it? No.

The responsible person is always a doer, and the doer is brave. They know that they have free will, endless choices and the opportunity to shape their future. They take ownership of the problem and look for solutions regardless of who caused the problem in the first place. Now that is brave.

It is also brave to admit when you have made a mistake. It is not brave to pretend it has never happened and hope it will disappear on its own or even worse, lay the blame on someone else. If you recall, all mistakes are lessons. There is no shame in making a mistake or seeing that you could have done something differently. In fact, it is liberating and it is something that should be celebrated, not punished. Mistakes = lessons = growth = success. Plain and simple. Admitting a mistake is a brave thing to do and should be acknowledged, not punished.

Conscious leaders are brave by virtue of the fact that they take on all challenges and respond in ways that foster inspiration and growth. They are brave because they put themselves in a position of control and influence. They are brave because they behave honourably and transparently at all times. They are brave because they are committed to their values, to their teams and to their purpose. They care about people and the environment and the impact they have on both. They are brave because they are not shy to admit an error nor are they afraid to take the heat. Their bravery leads them to success time and time again because with such an approach there is certainly no room for failure.

Just over 10 years ago I attended a management training course. My then employer believed (rightly so) that all the managers in the office (there were 8 of us at the time) could benefit greatly from this 3-day intensive, interactive workshop. It was indeed very useful and extremely interesting, but I will never forget one of the group activities which really opened my eyes and changed my way of thinking. We had to stand in a circle and each one of us had to say out loud 'I've made a mistake' and the others had to clap and cheer us on. I remember thinking what a brilliant exercise this was. What a way to break out of that traditional mind-set where responsibility is punished and blame and innocence is rewarded. So, when the first person's turn came to say, 'I've made a mistake', 3 managers in the group did not clap. I was shocked – these were my colleagues, people I interacted with daily and who, together with myself, were responsible for managing a team of 80 employees. The trainer turned and asked why they did not clap. The general response from all 3 was "why would I clap if someone has made a mistake? That is not something to reward or be happy about – that is something that should be frowned upon and where repercussions should follow". Wow. Talk about missing the mark. Over 10 years have passed and I have not forgotten that day, nor how their response made me feel (which was quite awful needless to say). It is brave to say that you have made a mistake and even braver to clap and say well done – now you have learnt from this experience and thank you for sharing it with me. That is the unconditional responsibility of the brave leader.

∞

"Do not lose sight of why you started in this line of business in the first place. Remember your values, be ethical and operate with social transparency. Take responsibility for all you say, think and do."

∞

Success

What does success mean to you? The definition changes all the time, doesn't it? I mean what do you do when you become 'successful' – you move on to the next thing that will make you 'successful'. Or can you ever become 'successful' if there is not a finite success that you are striving towards?

I believe society has a warped view of success. We are quick to call someone with fame and fortune successful and everyone else 'not' but is that what success means? And if these people have acquired what we consider to be 'success' why are they still pushing forward and why have they not stopped and retreated with their fame and fortunes to spend their days lounging by their pools? How many times have you heard about someone 'falling from grace' and no longer being at the 'pinnacle' – whatever that means.

Success is, just like time, relative to the observer. And it is a process, not a destination. We are successful every single day. When we watch our children dress themselves for the first time – we count that as a success. When we close a deal we had been working on for a long time – we count that as a success. When we receive our first paying client – we count that as a success. So, you see, success is not one particular fixed event. It is happening all the time, all around us, to all of us and in different, subjective ways.

As success cannot be defined objectively, give it your own definition. For some people, making it through the day counts as the biggest success there is. Think back to a time when you were grieving the loss of someone you loved. Was it a success to survive that day's emotions and pain and grief? Indeed, it was. For others, success means accomplishing something on their bucket list – a trip to an exotic destination or climbing a mountain peak. Whatever it is, the key to success is to recognise each small milestone as a success and celebrate it as a show of gratitude.

Because every success is but a moment in time. It is a feeling – a sense of achievement united with a specific event. Once that has been attained, we give thanks and celebrate and then move forward to the next one. You do not have to wait for 'fame and fortune' to feel successful. You are already successful. You create successful events every single day.

There is no such thing as failure. Really there isn't. Even if something does not work out, it is not a failure – it is a lesson on how to do it differently to achieve a different outcome. When you get the result you wanted, then it immediately moves from a lesson to a success.

When you shift your perception to look at it this way, how does that make you feel? Good right? And so it should. Remember that we are all here to provide something unique and value laden to the rest of the world. So how could there possibly be room for failure? No – there is room for learning and success. And all the other amazing things we experience in between.

Conscious leaders view success as building blocks to achieving their purpose. They know that every little step along the way, in the right direction, is the embodiment of all the successes they could know. Creating teams filled with empowered, happy, committed people is a success. Having all those teams working in line with their values towards a common goal is another success. Having an endless stream of customers and a wonderful reputation in the marketplace is yet another success. But even the small trivial day-to-day tasks offer successes that should be acknowledged and celebrated.

Success is not what other people tell you it is – it is what you want it to be at any given time. It is a feeling, a sensation. It is not a fixed, observable and measurable tangible thing. You have the power to see your successes and be proud of your achievements. You have gotten this far, how is that not a success already?

∞

"You are successful every single day. There is no such thing as ultimate success and there is no such thing as failure. Success is the accomplishment of every event, big or small, that means something to you. It is but a moment in time – celebrate it."

∞

Happiness

"It isn't what you have or who you are or where you are or what you are doing that makes you happy or unhappy. It is what you think about it."

— **Dale Carnegie**

All we want in this life is to be happy. Another subjective feeling that cannot be interpreted by anyone else nor can it be created by anyone else. Only we have the tools we need to create our own happiness. Whatever that means for us. Happiness is one of our main pursuits, is it not? From the dawn of time, philosophers have been chasing this metaphorical rabbit down the rabbit hole looking for the answers. Like success, we often think of it as a destination. As a goal. Once I have a, b and c I will be happy. Once I have achieved x, y and z I will be happy.

Happiness is a state of mind. You can be happy without a, b and c or x, y and z. And you can choose to be happy all the time no matter what is going on around you. Your happiness is completely independent and unrelated to external events, circumstances or situations. Your happiness is something only you control.

You need a few things to help get you to a constant state of happiness. Things like love (self-love first and foremost) and peace (more on that later) though these are all intertwined and need each other to thrive. It helps to rid yourself of a few of those feelings that no longer serve you such as fear and to give the ego a rest as it is always focused on what is lacking. Give yourself a good dose of courage and bravery as you acknowledge all the good that you have and you give thanks.

Enter the mind-set of the learner, in control and empowered. When you are happy day in day out, things start to shift. You will change. You will see things from a different perspective. You will see people and things that no longer serve you fall away and be grateful for it. Others will attune to your new frequency and bring you even more happiness as you do them. And the happiness will expand and grow and infiltrate every single aspect of your life.

When your vibration changes so much that you are in a state of constant happiness, you can truly create the world of your dreams. And that includes where you work regardless of whether you are an employee or it is your business. When you are happy your team is happy, your management is happy, your colleagues are happy, your clients are happy, your customers are happy. Even when there is a disagreement or someone no longer wants to work with you, you will notice that they leave happily – not up in arms and with all guns blazing. They will say their piece and leave in peace. They will be happy about their decision and you will be happy about the way it transpired, whilst you may not agree or wish things were different, you can see the peace and freedom that being happy about it brings.

Happiness is wonderful – it is so liberating because you are not in the constant pursuit for something that is out of reach. You can create it yourself at anytime and anywhere. Moments and places and people can bring you happiness depending on how you perceive them. If you go on holiday and from the moment you arrive are feeling sad about the fact that you will have to leave, then there is no space for you to find happiness there. Instead if you only think about each moment that you are spending, each activity you are participating in and every new thing you see and experience as and when you do, then those things will bring you happiness.

Try to think back to when you were younger. Before you had to worry about money and jobs and status and being able to provide for yourself and your family. Remember when you were the one being taken care of? Can you recall then, during a period of your life which was relatively stress free what used to make you happy? Maybe not all the time, but even one thing? When you do recall that one event, close your eyes and see if you can send yourself back there. Travel with your mind into that particular memory. Relive it and try to understand what it is about that memory that makes you feel happy. Maybe it was when you received your much-wanted first pet, or when you were playing in the sea with your siblings. Whatever it is, you will be able to experience how a thought today, of a time that has passed, can make you feel the same happiness you felt when you were actually experiencing the event for the first time. This exercise proves in a very short and easy way how our thoughts – that only we can control – have the power to make us feel any emotion we choose, particularly that of happiness.

Now think of this question: are you happy with your job or your business? What does that really mean? What is the happiness that you should be feeling in this situation or in this environment? If you feel comfortable where you are and are challenged, supported, valued and respected then that should help you to feel happy correct? Maybe yes, maybe no. How many times have you heard people tell you that they handed in their resignation and their superiors were shocked. That they were told that they thought they were happy, that they were paid well, that they were on the path to promotion? So why would they want to leave? Because happiness to them is defined in different terms than happiness is to you.

This is why conscious businesses are listening and adapting and creating environments where people are able to give and take and grow into at their own pace and with their own needs. They carve out roles and create space so that each person can adapt their position to find their own happiness. And happy team members are engaged, committed and purpose driven. They take ownership and responsibility just as happy conscious leaders do. And your bottom line can only thank you for it. There is no other way.

Happiness is everywhere if you can just open your eyes and look clearly at things. It is difficult when things do not go as you planned or if something or someone drops out of your life but these are not things you can control. And your happiness does not depend on these external factors. That is not to say that you will not experience events that make you unhappy. That is a part of life. But when you know that whether you continue to feel unhappy or happy lies in how and what you are thinking – that is the power and the beauty of being able to switch to happiness every single time.

Events that have happened in the past are over. Your thoughts of those events in the present are simply thoughts of events long gone. You can change your thoughts and therefore change your feeling about an event. Life is so precious that there is no reason to spend it unhappy. Look for the happiness within you and around you and you will understand how you hold the key in the pursuit of what makes your soul smile.

∞

"Conscious leaders are focused, clear, aware, present and purpose driven at all times. They know that to achieve this they must first look within. When we work from the inside out we open the doors to happiness and success at every level. Never has it been more important to sit in stillness and look within."

∞

Faith

"Believe in yourself. Have faith in your abilities. Without a humble but reasonable confidence in your own powers you cannot be successful or happy."
– Norman Vincent Peale

How many people truly believe in themselves and have faith in their ideas, intuition or abilities? Unfortunately, not enough. We often speak about faith in different contexts whether that is faith in a higher power or faith in your family or faith in your beliefs. But what about faith in yourself?
Having faith in yourself is another expression of self-love and of course any thoughts you have that you may not be good enough always get in the way. There is no one better at sabotaging your efforts than yourself.

So, what does having faith in yourself mean? It means that you have an unwavering and unmoveable belief that your dreams are right for you and no matter what, you can achieve them. You see all obstacles as challenges, all criticisms as constructive and all judgments as more reason to keep pushing forward. You trust your intuition – your 'gut' feelings. Innovation is born from within and no one can take that from you. You create your offering and if your market does not yet exist you can create that too. No one needed an iPod before they were created, no one needed a smartphone before they were created. But suddenly they existed and we all needed them as though our lives depended on them.

Know this for certain – you are capable of anything you put your mind to. It is not cliché, it is fact. Whatever you want to achieve or do or create you can do so by believing that you can. Put in the work required, make the sacrifices needed and you can move mountains (okay the last one maybe figuratively though life never ceases to amaze me!)

We are creative, courageous beings with the ability to think, inspire, build and materialise all that we want in this life. We need to really believe that we can do this and have faith in ourselves as a first step.

One thing I have learnt along the years is that there are people who may not like you – maybe a little, maybe not at all. There are people who may not agree with you and try to change your mind. There are people who will listen with interest as you share your dreams and then shut you down the minute you stop speaking. There are people who will criticise you for what you are about to do and try to make you stop. There are people who will look at you as though you have lost your marbles when you talk about your innovative idea. And of course, there are the people whose glass is always half empty and therefore so is everyone else's. As Albert Einstein said, 'stay away from negative people, they have a problem for every solution'.

Just remember – greatness never came from living a mediocre life. People did not invent amazing new things by being content with what was already in existence. Successful entrepreneurs did not stop even when they had to sleep in their cars. And you know why? Because they had faith. Faith in themselves and in their vision and in that voice in their head that told them that they could do it because they had to do it. They were put on this earth to disrupt and create. They knew that they could not be wrong and they knew it even when they had run out of money and were on their last few dollars not knowing how they would get through the next day.

What got them through was faith. Even if things do not go as planned, even if you have to start from scratch, even if you have to take a different road to get you there, when you have faith in yourself, in others and in the universe, you can never go wrong.

Conscious leaders know all about faith. They know about having faith in themselves and faith in their teams. They have faith in their ideas and in their ultimate goals. They know that by having faith in their people they are providing them with the forum to express themselves and to be creative. They are giving them the courage to speak up, to share and to take calculated risks. The faith they radiate affects everyone around them. If they are so confident then they must be on to something. If they are so sure of themselves then they must be right. Faith boosts self-esteem and boosts teamwork. It is the glue that holds the team together. When your boss has faith in you, how do you feel? You feel proud and resolute in proving them right. You work with your eyes on the goal with focus and clarity. Because you have faith that they have faith in you, you stir the universe into action to support and guide your every step. This is the power of faith.

∞

"To be a great leader, you must first see, acknowledge and nurture the greatness within. Have faith in your abilities and in your power. Make your internal brand so powerful, your external brand sells itself."

∞

Freedom

"Every human has four endowments – self-awareness, conscience, independent will and creative imagination. These give us the ultimate human freedom. The power to choose, to respond, to change."
— **Stephen Covey**

When we have understood love in all its different forms, together with the other elements we have touched upon so far, then we can start to feel the beauty of freedom.

What does freedom mean to you? To be free there must not be any coercions or constraints. To be free you must be able to think, say and do as you please, without controls and without limitations being imposed on you. To be free you must be free to move around without confinement. Some of these we can guarantee for everyone, others we cannot. But the one thing that is always free and that can never be restricted is our ability to think. Our thoughts, by virtue of them being in our minds, are free. What you think about will also determine the freedom that you will feel.

Freedom is another journey that we embark on – moments can make you feel as though you have mastered it, other moments may have you struggling for air. You know the feeling. First day of holidays, stepping your feet into the waves and feeling the coolness of the water against your ankles and the sand in between your toes. For that moment in time you have forgotten all the worries of the world and all the weight on your shoulders has lifted. For that moment in time you are free – you just exist right there and then in that freeze frame and you know that life is fabulous. Sitting amongst a pile of unpaid bills on the other hand does not give you the same feeling – it is in that moment in time that you feel you are trapped with no way out. Anything but free. But these are again snap shots in time and it is our interpretation of them that will determine how free we feel.

When you can really live in your presence and in your awareness of self, you are free. Within this heightened sense of being you can feel the absolute freedom that is, because in each moment there is nothing but that instant in space-time. And in that instant, there is nothing but you – the real you – and the real you is always free.

With freedom comes the power to be who you want to be and to fulfil your dreams without any limitations. With freedom also comes an enhanced self-awareness and knowledge about who you are and what you stand for. To succeed in business and as a conscious leader you really have to have mastered the act of being and feeling free.

Conscious leaders who feel free do not have to give in to their ego or fear, instead they can speak and act without any self-doubt. They are as we say – fearless – because they are free. They inspire and lead and create greatness just by being who they are. They are a living, walking example of everything they hold dear and value and their actions will always support any words that come out of their mouths. They create an environment of infinite possibilities because they vibrate at the energy of freedom. Freedom from constraints and limitations. Freedom from anxiety and anger. Freedom from victimisation and resentment. Freedom to make mistakes and acknowledge them. Freedom to accept constructive criticism and listen to other viewpoints. Freedom to know that they are who they are and within that lies their power.

You have a gift. Every one of us does. You can do something differently and more effectively than someone else. That is not to make life into a competition, but to point out your power and your ability to make a difference. You can think in a different way and act in a different way regardless of what is going on around you. Take a stance for what you hold dear, take that big leap of faith into the unknown and try something new. Create and live the life you have always dreamed about. You have that freedom and you have had it all along. Do not settle for a mediocre life filled with unfulfilled dreams and desires. Take charge now.

Look at yourself and acknowledge the greatness within you. Take the steps you need to achieve self-love and to get to know who you really are. Focus on learning and growing and becoming better at everything you think, say and do. Strive for an excellence that means something to you, not to society. See how lucky you are daily, see how events and circumstances can help you develop your skills and your abilities. Recognise your capabilities and the power you have to change your world and the world of those around you and beyond. Give in to the freedom of your thoughts and the limitless world that you can create in your mind. What you focus on and what you visualise will become your reality. Steep your creations in love and freedom. Get excited and be inspired and show people around you how simple steps can create greatness at all levels. Be at one with yourself. Learn to listen and to love and to respect every person's freedom at all times. Free yourself from judgment and things you 'should do' – recognise that there is nothing you 'should do' but only what you 'want to do'. You have free will and freedom of thought. That can never be taken from you. Be sure to never forget that.

∞

"Your thoughts become your self-fulfilling prophecy.
Think big, think change, think success, think freedom and
be who you want to be."

∞

Love and Peace
(B-Side)

∞

"When the power of love overcomes the love of power the world will know peace."

— **Jimi Hendrix**

∞

We end our journey right where we began – with love. The one driving force, governing all the things we have spoken about and propelling us forward, whether we realise it or not, to become better human beings. In tune with ourselves, the earth and the universe. Feeling love for all irrespective of race, sex, religion, opinion or belief system. Being at peace with who we are and who is around us. In a perfect world this is how it should be. But do not be disheartened. As we know, we hold the power to implement and create massive change within ourselves and in the world around us every single day.

Peace must begin with us. Internal peace. Peace within our souls, within our beings. Love has the power to get us there. Self-love, respect and honouring – who we are and what we are here to do will start the process. Freedom, courage and living our truth give us power and control over our lives and this also leads to inner peace. Being happy with our choices, the outcomes and our path enhances the feeling of peace within. You can now see the importance of each element we have looked at within this guide – individually and holistically. We are planting the first seedlings of change. We are tuning our minds to a different channel – a different way of doing things. We are freeing ourselves from years and years of conditioning and archaic methods that no longer work. We are starting to really look within as we realise that everything we want is already available to us. Every change we want to create is already in our hands ready to be implemented. Every opportunity to excel is already at our doorstep. And this is why we start by going within, because without the core work, we are unable to grasp the greatness that lies beyond. Through strengthening our core, much like any exercise practice, we are able to empower ourselves as brave conscious leaders.

If we trusted in the power of love and allowed it to seep through into everything we think, say and do, we would start to shift the energy within and of those around us and eventually they would do the same.

Imagine a world where there is respect and understanding and love and peace. Would you like to live in a world like that? Then start small. Create that world in your own body first by controlling the mind, then in your home, then in your workplace and eventually something will start to move, to change. Be aware of the world around you and your impact within it, daily. What you eat, what you wear, what you buy, what activity you engage in – try to see it from a different standpoint. Try to see it as though for the first time. Where do you fit in? See if you can start to buy your products from ethical sources that look after human and animal life and the environment you live in. Try to release yourself from the binds of materialism as you free yourself from things you do not need. Focus on building strong relationships with others instead based on mutual respect, trust and love.

Be brave in the pursuit of your dreams and give thanks for the opportunities that come your way. Life is as beautiful and inspiring and amazing as you will it to be when you can really see it for what it is. Love will get you there and with that knowledge you will acquire a peace you never thought possible.

And you will revel in that peace, as an empowered human being, out there ready to change the world for the better. So, go on, what are you waiting for? The time to start is now.

∞

"Focus on love – it is the highest and purest of all vibrations. It leads you to peace, freedom, bliss and harmony."

∞